Published in the United States
by Xist Publishing
www.xistpublishing.com
PO Box 61593 Irvine, CA 92602

Hardcover ISBN: 978-1-5324-2964-4
Paperback ISBN: 978-1-5324-2963-7
eISBN: 978-1-5324-2962-0

Printed in the USA

xist Publishing

Knock, Knock, Monster Who?

(Illustrated Monster Jokes for Kids)

Stephanie
Rodriguez

Adam
Pryce

xist Publishing

What do little monsters like to ride on at the amusement park?

The scary-go-round!

What does a monster do when he loses his head?

He calls a head hunter.

How did the monster cure his sore throat?

He spent all day gargoyling.

How do monsters begin fairy tales?

"Once upon a slime . . ."

Who is the messiest monster?

Slopzilla!

What do sea monsters have for dinner?

Fish and ships.

Why is the monsters' basketball court wet?

Because the players keep dribbling on it.

What does the hungry monster get after he's eaten too much ice cream?

More ice cream!

What's creepy and leads to the second floor of a haunted house?

Monstairs!

Knock Knock.
Who's there?
Gargoyle.

Gargoyle Who?

If you Gargoyle with saltwater, your throat will feel better!

What should you do if a monster runs through your front door?

Run through the back door.

Why was the monster feeling sick?

It ate some vegetables!

What do you do with a green monster?

Put it in the sun until it ripens!

What vampire is always eating junk food?

Snackula!

What makes an ideal present for a monster?

Five pairs of gloves.

Knock Knock.
Who's there?
Monster.
Monster who?

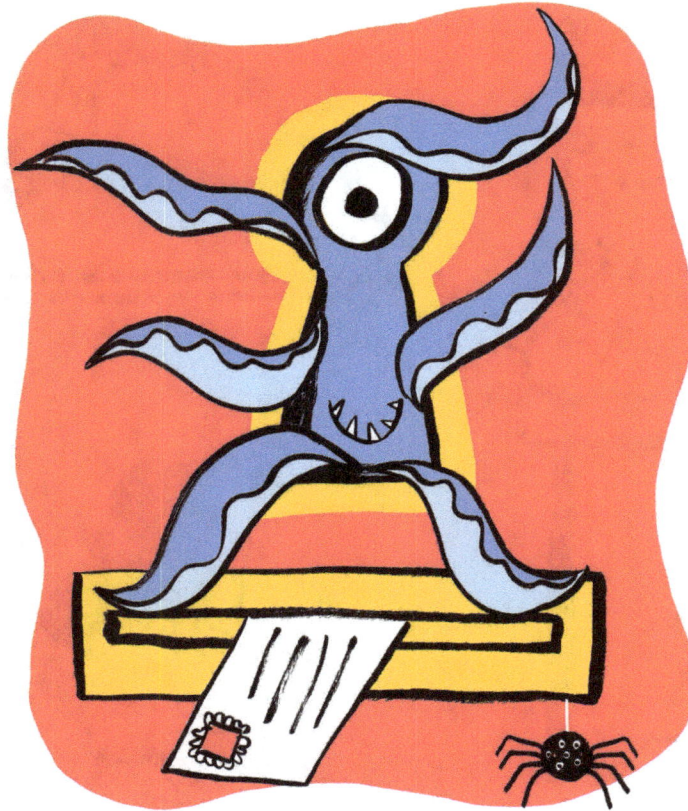

Do you really want to know who the monster is at your door?

What's a monster's favorite play?

Romeo and Ghouliet.

What is the best way to speak to a monster?

From a long distance away!

What time is it when a monster sits on your car?

Time to buy a new one!

Why did the monster knit herself three socks?

Because she had three feet.

What do monsters turn on during the summer?

The scare conditioner.

What type of monster loves dance music?

The boogeyman.

What kind of car do huge monsters drive?

A monster truck.

What kind of monster has two mouths?

The one with two heads.

Don't Miss the other Illustrated Jokes books from xist Publishing

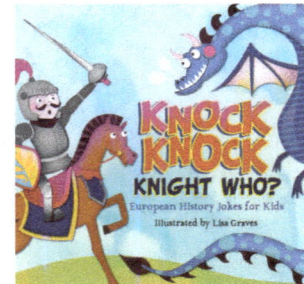

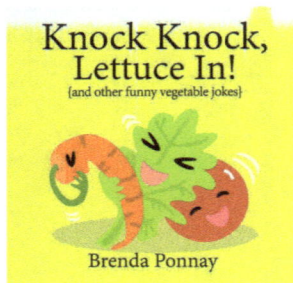

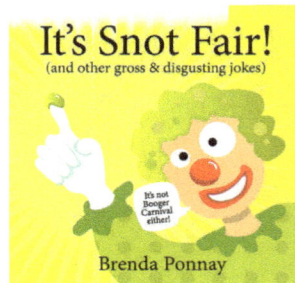

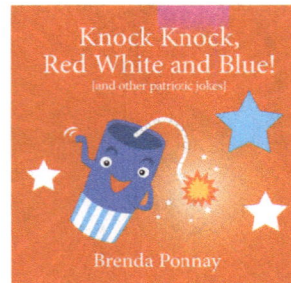

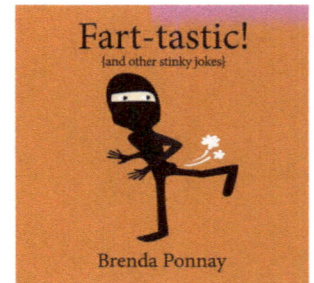

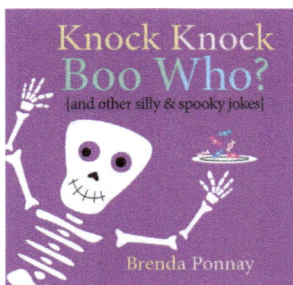

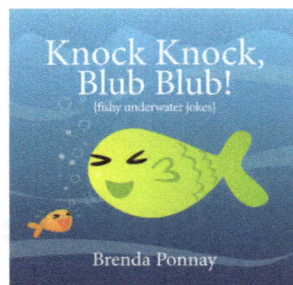

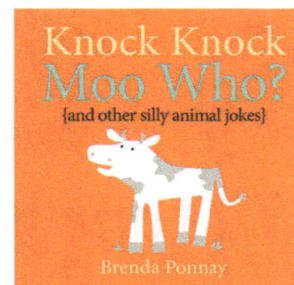

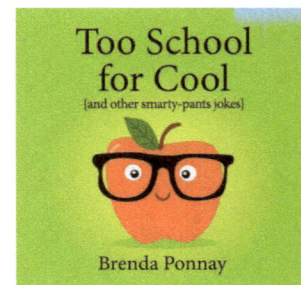

KNOCK-KNOCK DINO-MITE!
(DINOSAUR JOKES FOR KIDS)
CHRIS ROBERTSON

KNOCK KNOCK KNIGHT WHO?
European History Jokes for Kids
Illustrated by Lisa Graves

Knock Knock, Lettuce In!
{and other funny vegetable jokes}
Brenda Ponnay

It's Snot Fair!
(and other gross & disgusting jokes)
It's not Booger Carnival either!
Brenda Ponnay

Knock Knock, Red White and Blue!
{and other patriotic jokes}
Brenda Ponnay

Fart-tastic!
{and other stinky jokes}
Brenda Ponnay

Knock Knock Boo Who?
{and other silly & spooky jokes}
Brenda Ponnay

Knock Knock, Blub Blub!
{fishy underwater jokes}
Brenda Ponnay

Knock Knock Moo Who?
{and other silly animal jokes}
Brenda Ponnay

Too School for Cool
{and other smarty-pants jokes}
Brenda Ponnay

www.ingramcontent.com/pod-product-compliance
Lightning Source LLC
LaVergne TN
LVHW082324080426
835508LV00042B/1537